Chapter 1 Background And Strategic Location

The Denver International Airport, (Den) or DIA, is the largest
airport in the United States by total land area, 35,000 acres, which opened on

February 28, 1995. By 2016, Denver became the 18th busiest airport in the world, with US passenger traffic of over 58 million passengers. It is the primary hub for Great Lakes Airlines, and Frontier Airlines, as well as Southwest Airlines and United Airlines. An arched curvature steel cable system supports the fabric peaked roof comprised of Teflon coated fiberglass material. It is notable for its reflection of snow capped mountains. Theorists claim this design was meant to be representative of Indian teepees, as the airport is centered on an Indian burial ground site. DIA is one of the world's greenest airports, and has constructed the largest solar farm located at a commercial airport in the US.

This airport is approximately 25 miles from downtown Denver, further away than Stapleton Airport which it replaced. The justification for the new Denver International Airport strategic location was chosen to avoid loud aircraft noise disrupting industrialized areas, the ability to accommodate more generous runway layouts not complicated by severe weather conditions, and to allow for further growth and expansion. The gate space at Stapleton Airport had been severely limited. Its runways were not able to effectively cope with Denver's unpredictable weather patterns and winds, which resulted in national travel disruptions.

The construction schedule on the airport was delayed 16 months behind schedule, at a cost of two billion over budget. These increases were due to changes in the sizing of the airport, widening and lengthening concourses, and installing an automated baggage system, that never performed to expectations. Former airport construction workers stated they were behind schedule because there were five multistory buildings that were built underneath the airport, creating a complex networking of tunnels that lie beneath the airport. These underground tunnels being central to the airport's rail system. Additionally, there were constant construction changes, and mass terminations of teams once they had completed their section of work. Thus, it is reported that no one group attained the final blueprint of the airport.

This project began with Perez Architects, and was finished by Fentress Bradburn Architects, Pouw & Associates, and Bruton & Associates, at a final cost of 4.8 billion dollars. There is a massive pile of dirt that is masked as a landfill that is visible exceeding 300' in altitude. It is claimed that the FAA felt this would be dangerous to travelers and could be a potential radar issue that could cause a disaster. The addition of this dirt was to be gradual process over a lengthy time frame, however it was completed in 4 years, without explanation.

Funding for the airport was submitted by The New World Order Commission, supposedly a group of Denver businessmen and civic leaders that were responsible as sponsors and organizers of some of the events, that occurred at the airport opening. However, no records exist for this organization. A large portion of the Denver Airport is referenced as the "Great Hall", named after a room found in Freemason lodges of secret societies.

Conspiracy theorists claim the new Denver International Airport was not popular with the local people, and truly not needed. The exuberant amount of money spent on this structure, and the masonic imagery leads them to believe it could be a base for The New World Order command bunkers, fallout shelters, or future Fema camps for interment of dissident citizens. Factually, The Denver International Airport is a part of a Continuity of Government Program and does state it houses an underground facility. Skeptics of these theories proclaim that the city of Denver wanted to construct an airport for expansion purposes to accommodate the midfield terminal and its concourses.

The Denver International Airport

Interior Of The Denver International Airport

Chapter 2 Conspiracy Theories Of The DIA

On the surface, Denver International is a large modern airport that services millions upon millions of passengers each year, domestically and internationally. However, conspiracy theories abound as to the true significance behind this airport, as it is surrounded by a barbed wire guard fence, and barren acres of fenced lots, reportedly for safety reasons. The theorists proclaim the barbed wire is angled inward as if to keep people inside, not out as in other airports, as a future military base for Fema camps. Skeptics do not adhere to this, as they say there is no difference in the fencing, it sticks out and up, as in any other commercial airport. Thus, the speculation continues on this matter, as multiple people can view the same object, and perceive it from different viewpoints.

In February 2007, in the early afternoon, at least 14 planes mysteriously experienced cracked windshields. Some of them were taking off, others were landing, and the remaining ones were parked in the airfield. The airport weather at that time was a mixture of rapid temperature changes and high winds and snow. Some officials indicated the windshield damages could be attributed to ice or blowing debris. Another possibility they suggested was that a power surge could have occurred affecting the electronically heated windshields, when the airplanes were connected to the auxiliary power lines at the gates. The NTSB concluded it was fine particles of debris and high winds, but the exact nature of this debris was undetermined.

There were reports of electronic and magnetic vibrations which made some people sick and gave others headaches. The conspiracy theory of this event is that the spontaneously shattered windshields were the result of electromagnetic pulses. supposedly caused by a nuclear explosion underground or some type of secret underground testing. Skeptics propose a magnetic pulse generally won't create a shock wave strong enough to break glass unless its caused by an open air explosion, but sonic waves could be produced by unknown devices that could shatter glass.

Five unidentified buildings were completed and buried with the explanation presented that they were constructed incorrectly. It is said that eight levels of underground facilities exist, and that this underground construction's purpose is for the underground train system that is a connection to all the terminals. They state that additional tunneling is being done for future expansion, as the workers report in and out of work each day without noticing anything unusual. There are mini cooling towers that vent the underground levels up to over 88 square miles deep.

Many theorists propose that this underground tunnel system leads to Norad at Cheyenne Mountain in Colorado Springs, Co. They insist it is a underground base for the US government during a catastrophic event, and these city sized bases could accommodate millions of people, as hidden fallout shelters, or bunkers. Others propose the theory it is a secret headquarters designed by The New World Order, Neo-Nazis or Reptoids. The New World Order agenda to control humanity through a global genocide, as indicated in the unnerving airport's murals, with the Australian antigen "AuAg". The Nazi reference refers to the organized swastika designed runways, when viewed aerially. The proposed Reptoids are shape shifting lizard people or aliens hiding under the airport, for eventual world domination. It has been reported that the Queen of England has been secretly purchasing the property that surrounds the airport by proxy.

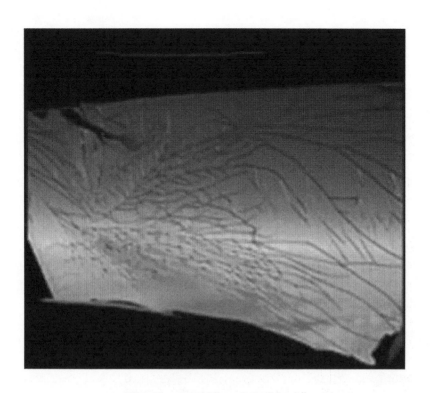

DIA Shattered Plane Windshield

Norad At Cheyenne Mountain Complex

Chapter 3 Ominous Annubis Statue/ Sinister Blue Mustang Sculpture

An immense monumental statue of Annubis, the ancient Egyptian god of the afterlife, stands south of the Jeppesen Terminal. In mythology, he presided over the valuables in the tombs of the pharaohs. This colored replica statue of massive dimensions, is 26 feet tall and weighs 7 tons. This piece of art with a jackal head was created to celebrate the King Tut Exhibit to the Denver Art Museum.

"Annubis" Statue

The Blue Mustang is a striking electric blue colored anatomically correct, cast fiberglass sculpture, that the locals have nicknamed "Blucifer". It has illuminated red glowing eyes, and is also referred to as the "Demon Horse", "Devil Horse", and the "Blue Stallion of Death". It is claimed that its eyes are a tribute from the artist to his father, whose vocation had been a neon sign maker. Located along Pena Boulevard, the main road to the airport, the statue has received great public attention and petitions to remove it, some deeming it creepy and embarrassing, while others view it as amazing.

It was commissioned as public art for the airport, with the horse representing the uncivilized fortitude of the Old American West. However it has come to symbolize death, as it killed its creator, Luis Jimenez, when a section of it fell on him severing an artery in his leg in 2006. The sculpture was then completed by his staff, family, and professional race car painters. This 32 foot tall sculpture weighing 9,000 lbs. was unveiled at the Denver International Airport on February 11, 2008. This centerpiece of intrigue had been commissioned in 1993, for a price of 300,000.

Supposedly, this mustang was based on a lesser similar sculpture by Jimenez named "Mesteno", he created at the University of Oklahoma, depicting the spirit of the uncultivated determination of the West in the shape of a midnight blue stallion. Conspiracy theories refer to the "Blucifer" statue as the horse of the apocalypse, the fourth horse noted in the book of Revelation in the Bible, referred to as "Death".

Blue Mustang Sculpture

"Mesteno"

Chapter 4 Bizzarre Murals And Inexplicable Floor Markings

Two of the most highly debated artwork pieces in the airport are the murals, located in level 5 of the Jeppesen Terminal, created by the Mexican artist, Leo Tanguma. Their symbolic imagery of disturbing violence and destruction has gained suspicion behind their intentions. Theorists claim their themes illustrate annihilation events, future militant oppression, such as martial law, and a one world government. The murals are named "In Peace and Harmony with Nature," and "The Children of the World Dream of Peace". Tanguma insists that the murals were not meant to be frightening, their meanings concern environmentalism, and preservation of the earth. He states they depict destruction of the environment, genocide, as well as mankind bonding together to heal nature and attain peace, thus the victory of peace over war.

In the mural "In Peace and Harmony with Nature", children are depicted with frightened looks on their faces, and plants and vegetation surround them. Their are flames of fire in the background overtaking a city, while a child holds a Mayan tablet that some suggests represents the end of the world. Additionally, there are coffins of deceased children, located at the bottom of the painting. The proposed meaning is that the world unites to conquer evil and bring peace to all.

"In Peace and Harmony with Nature"

In the mural of "The Children of the World Dream of Peace", is a two part piece, one of content kids holding national flags above a Nazi soldier wearing a gas mask. The second part of the painting features this sinister soldier carrying a machine gun and sword, stabbing the white dove of peace surrounded by the ruins of a city. A child is sleeping with a teddy bear, while a woman is in tears holding a injured child. On the bottom right of the painting is a letter featured written by a young boy that was killed at the Auschwitz concentration camp of 1943. The soldier is seen as a figure of authority over the masses, for an event of the future.

"The Children of The World Dream of Peace"

"The Children of The World Dream of Peace"

On the tile floor in front of the above mural, is what resembles a cart that could be found in a gold mine with the inscription AuAg, believed to reference gold and silver. Conspiracy theorists claim that it represents a deadly hepatitis strain known as Australian Antigen, or a toxic gas that could be a powerful armament in genetic warfare wiping out the world's population.

Tile AuAg Marking

Unusual floor markings are visibly cut into the floor with their explanations presented as Masonic, Satanic, or some type of secret code. Theorists propose there are secret Nazi messages concerning the black sun drawing written on the floor. The floor motif depicts the sun, with the black disk preceding to eclipse it, as the black sun is known as the sun wheel in German. It is a symbol of mysterious occult importance, mostly in association with the Nazis.

Nazi Black Sun Drawing

The expression Dzit Dit Gaii, a Masonic design is inscribed on the airport floor. There are claims that this is a Navajo phrase referring to white mountain known as Mt. Blanc or the white mountain in France. This location being the site where the Knights of the Templar signed their freemasonry charter.

Baffling Floor Marking

Chapter 5 Cryptic Dedication Marker/ Eerie Gargoyle Suitcases

Located in the DIA's Great Hall, is the dedication marker capstone. The marker implies that the airport was commissioned by The New World Order Commission that has been discovered not to exist. It is inscribed with the compass symbol of freemasonry, listing two of the grand lodges of freemasonry in Colorado. The date of dedication was presented on March 19, 1994, and the marker is mounted over a time capsule that was sealed during this ceremony, stating not to be opened until 2094. Conspiracy theorists suggest that by adding all the numbers together of the dedication date, the result is the number 33, which in freemasonry is symbolic of the highest degree and perfection.

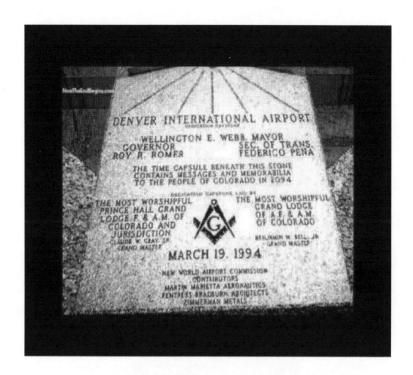

Dedication Marker Capstone

There is a brass plaque at the end of the curved pedestal located above the time capsule. This plaque represents a Masonic symbol, the remainder of the text from the time capsule is written in Braille. There are those that believe this keypad can be accessed with a code that can perhaps unlock the capsule, permit admittance to the underground bases, or may trigger a universal genocide predicament.

Brass Plaque with Keypad/ Time Capsule

In the east and west baggage claim areas are a pair of gargoyles that are perched inside suitcases, ensuring the safe arrival of baggage. Historically speaking, Gargoyles were placed on buildings to protect and guard that site, by defending against evil spirits. The Freemasons were builders of many temples in Europe, and conspiracy theories propose the Denver International Airport is a temple or cathedral symbolic for the Masons, and The New World Order. Others say gargoyles are symbolic of reptilian aliens that reside in the underground bases beneath the airport.

"Demon" Gargoyle in Suitcase

Chapter 6 Mysterious Runway Designs/ Bunkers/ Tunnels

The Denver International Airport is surrounded by runways connected to them with taxiways. Planes can arrive and depart simultaneously with better efficiency, with six non intersecting runways, with a divided airfield between east and west sides. The runway layouts are perpendicular , not running parallel to one another. This extra distance provides ample room around other aircraft in inclement weather. There are claims that a secret runway has been buried just inches underneath the dirt at this facility. Some conspiracy theorists claim the runway patterns are organized in the shape of a Nazi Swastika when viewed aerially, that is representative of a Neo-Nazi future domination. Others believe there are no sinister runway patterns, that the runway designs resemble a pinwheel form.

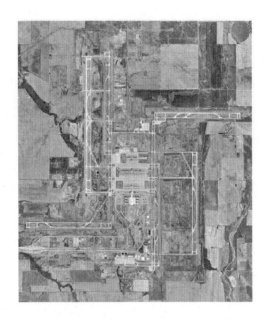

DIA Runway Designs

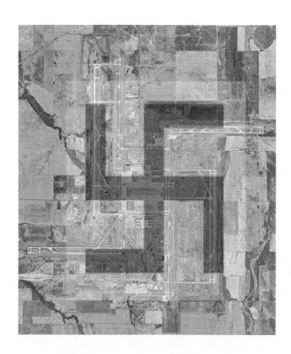

Swastika DIA Runways

      The most prominent conspiracy theory of the Denver International Airport is that there is a doomsday bunker or underground CIA base, to be utilized as headquarters for The New World Order Government. The New World Order goals are for a one world government, one world religion, a one world currency, and a mass depopulation and Agenda 21, with the remaining survivors micro chipped for control and tracking purposes.The strange symbols and markings and fateful imagery at the airport seem to predicate a theme for a catastrophic future event.

      It has been proposed there are five giant government bases buried under the airport, that presumably travels down for over 8 levels. These underground buildings with a proposed depth from 75 to 120 feet for each, and have interconnecting tunnels to each other, and a 40 foot diameter tunnel as well. This secret military city being full of workers, and aliens, and vehicles, for purposes of medical research laboratories, work camps, prisoner facilities, and military accommodations and food storage.

This underground airport of one million square feet along with two 7,000 feet tunnels form a complex of highways, bullet trains, and roads that connect with a secret network of cities, governmental facilities, and military bases across the nation. Most areas are not in use, like dead baggage equipment, chain link fences, and locked fences leading to lower levels. Whistle blowers have stated that there is equipment located underground with automated and segregated gates and door mechanisms. The area is patrolled by police officers, and there are tugs and carts due to the fact the automated baggage system is no longer in use.

The theory is that Denver has been chosen as the new capitol for the United States, chosen for its high elevation, centralized location, and its secretive rocky terrain, and its private underground location. The CIA Langley headquarters in Virginia, made plans to relocate to Denver for its domestic division, responsible for operational procedures in the US. Skeptics debunk this theory as they say the massive tunnel system underneath the airport is used for the giant transit system for the airport as well as the baggage transport system, for the tunnels provide typical baggage handling systems.

Underground View of Denver International Airport

Secret Underground Base DIA

One of the most commonly asked questions concerning
these hypothesized theories, is why anyone would be so blatant to expose
their agenda in public with symbols and imagery. The answer can be found in
the New World Order code, their belief that before your destroy your enemy,
you must alert them to your plans, through symbolism or clues. They enforce
their power and wealth in public through occult imagery and hand signals,
and subliminal messages in videos and songs. They reveal different aspects
of their plans through blockbuster Hollywood movies, books, television, and
signs or symbolism.Their motivation is to attain more power and control, to
brainwash the masses with their beliefs, and to reduce the population to a
sustainable level. Those that are not members of their organization are

considered weak and expendable workers.

This global elite secret society, shadow government, the "Illuminati," rule the world through their great wealth with assets that are more than the combined funds of the world. Their 13 bloodline families within the organization control the Cabal, the Astor, Bundy, Collins, DuPont, Freeman, Kennedy, Li, Onassis, Reynolds, Rockefeller, Rothschild, Russell, and Van Duyn bloodlines. Its members are the most powerful bankers, entertainers, politicians, financiers, and business people of the world, and are included in the exclusive Bilderberg group. The Bilderberg group is an organization that meets once or twice a year at remote locations, no reporters are allowed on the premises, and no one knows the member list, except for other members.They manipulate the world's economies and markets, control the mainstream media's news, control wars and politicians, and keep everyone under surveillance, experimenting with new types of mind control. They are perfecting cloning technology techniques to allow them to replace anyone. The Bohemian Grove is their retreat and it is claimed that they are occult worshipers of the statue of a gigantic owl there.

Their code stipulates that everything must be in balance, as negative acts must be accompanied by positive ones, as the super rich will make enormous donations to philanthropic charities. They are master manipulators that control and influence every major corporation or organization in all technologically advanced countries directly, or by proxy vote. Their members hold high level positions in key corporations and institutions, allowing doors to be opened and infiltrated by more of their kind. The most influential members are occult specialists that initiate major events, or false flag attacks, on days of occult significance. Biblical prophesy attributes The New World Order , to Luciferian Freemasons,under the control of the Antichrist, who ushers in the end times with the false messiah, and the final battle Armageddon, good against evil, that leads to Satan's defeat.

Illuminati New World Order (All-Seeing Eye of Horus)

In conclusion, the Denver International Airport holds a unique status in its notoriety and controversy of a commercial airport in the world. Sometimes the truth may be stranger than fiction, even if it seems unbelievable and shocking. Theorists insist why all the secrecy, symbols, and prophetic imagery if there is no nefarious agenda. This book has presented the history and background of the airport, the conspiracy theories and probable explanations for them, and the factual evidence of symbolic artwork, and imagery, and the concepts of the secret society of The New World Order. I encourage all my readers to access further research , as this introduction to the DIA has only highlighted the main points of interest. It is up to each individual to analyze fact from fiction, arriving at their own personal conclusions, by being well-informed, attaining knowledge and insight, to possibly avert perilous times for our future by being prepared, to survive and live in peace.

Cheryl Leonard

Conspiracy Theories

Post Apocalyptic Monument
The Georgia Guidestones

Conspiracy Theories

Post Apocalyptic Monument

The Georgia Guidestones

On the highest elevation in Elbert County, Georgia near the South Carolina border, towers a megalithic granite monument known as The Georgia Guidestones, sometimes referred to as "The American Stonehenge," due to striking resemblances to each other. This mysterious doomsday inscribed structure, portends written messages of directions for humanity, after the events of an apocalypse. The true identity of the man who referred to himself as R.C. Christian (a pseudonym), and was responsible for the commission of its construction is unknown, as well as the group of secret associates he represented. This book summarizes an insightful look into this intriguing puzzle of its origin, architectural features, commandments/ languages, the inferences to Thomas Paine's "Age of Reason", conspiracy theories, and the mysterious cube inscriptions in 2014.

Chapter 1 Origin Of The Georgia Guidestones

Chapter 2 Architectural Layout Of The Cryptic Monument

Chapter 3 The Ten Commandments/ Eight Languages/Ancient Texts

Chapter 4 Thomas Paine "The Age of Reason"

Chapter 5 Theories/ Mysterious Cube Inscriptions 2014

Chapter 1 Origin Of The Georgia Guidestones

The story begins in June 1979, when a well dressed gentleman supposedly reported in the range of middle aged up to his 70's, entered the office of the Elberton Granite Finishing Company, in Elberton, Georgia. He referred to himself as R.C. Christian, admitting his name was a pseudonym, and that he was representing a small group of loyal Americans that believed in God, and wanted to build a monument for the conservation of mankind for future generations. His true name and their names in his organization still remain unknown today, and conspiracy theorists state that this wisdom for humanity is shrouded in pagan overtones and occult philosophy.

R.C. Christian has been referenced to 1st Frater C.R.C. later known as Christian RosenKreuz, with the English name being Christian Rose Cross, who was the legendary founder of the Rosicrucian Order. Rosicrucians were followers of the religious order of the Rosy Cross. They were alluded to as a secret society of mystics in late medieval Germany who claimed to possess inner secret truths concerning the universe, nature and the spiritual realm. They have been linked in association with the Knights Templar and the Freemasons. The concept of God in the secret societies of freemasonry is referred to as "The Great Architect", a substitution for the divine one true God.

Christian spoke to the President of Elberton Granite Finishing Company, Joe H Fendley Sr, and told him of his mission plans for the monument to be commissioned. Christian claimed the Elbert county area was chosen as his location site for the monument due to its abundant supply of top grade granite, its rural landscape, and mild climate. Fendley tried to discourage Christian, and was shocked by his story, so he quoted him an exorbitant price explaining the building of the monument would require specialty tools, paid consultants, and the use of heavy equipment. He sent Christian to Wyatt Martin, who was the President of Granite City Bank.

Wyatt Martin (Right) President Granite City Bank

Joe Fendley Sr. Builder Georgia Guidestones

Martin found Christian to be educated, well-spoken, possibly a world traveler and environmentalist, as he explained to him that his group had been planning the construction of this monument for 20 years, and that they wished to remain anonymous forever. Martin told him he had to verify the man's true identity, to proceed, so he could rest assured he would be able to fund this project. They were able to negotiate an agreement, in which Christian would reveal his true identity, and Martin would sign a nondisclosure agreement that he would never discuss the information with anyone, and would destroy all the documents and records pertaining to the monument when it was completed.

Christian transferred money from different banks all over the country, leaving no trail that could be traced. Christian provided detailed instructions to Fendley for the size of the structure in specific metric measurements, and insisted that the structure be built to withstand an apocalypse, and provided a replica of a wooden model of the monument. He stated its purpose would be to function as a clock, calendar, and compass, by its alignment to the sun, stars, and the moon. Conspiracy theorists contend that occultists will worship alignment and movement of celestial bodies in their religious ceremonies.

The location site for the monument was a 5 acre plot owned by Wayne Mullinex,in which it is purported that Christian paid him $5,000, and granted lifetime grazing rights for the cattle of Mullinex and children. Mullinex's construction company supposedly laid the foundations for the Guidestones. After all transactions and instructions were concluded, Christian bid farewell to Fendley, saying to him, he would never see him again. Christian continued to correspond with Martin, sending letters from different cities from around the country, never from the same place. The last letter that Martin received was approximately at the time of the 911 terrorist attacks , and he has made the assumption that he has now passed away.

Martin is retired, and no longer resides in Elberton, he maintains that he cannot reveal the secret of the mystery man, as he made a promise he must keep to him. It has been reported that he did not destroy the documents and records pertaining to the document, and that they are being kept in his garage. After the Georgia Guidestones were unveiled on March, 22, 1980, the townspeople sparked controversy over the monument, referring to it as the devil's work, predicting occult groups would come to worship there, and that it was of satanic origin built by a Luciferian secret society. A sandblaster named Charlie Clamp claimed that when he was etching the lettering on the slabs, he heard unusual music and incoherent voices. These claims were due to the Antichrist ten commandments or messages, that many believe are inscribed on the monument. Today, Elberton has become a tourist attraction because of the fascination behind the Georgia Guidestones. Elbert County is the owner of the Georgia Guidestones site.

Chapter 2 Architectural Layout Of The Cryptic Monument

The Georgia Guidestones Monument is a highly engineering feat due to its attention to detail and specifications. The structure contains four gigantic blue granite slabs, one center stone referred to as the Gnomen Stone, and they share a capstone which aligns the top. These massive granite slabs have been erected to stand approximately 20 feet tall, and with a mass of 240,000 lbs. More than 4000 sandblasted letters and characters reveal eight languages and four ancient language scripts. On each face of these four upright stones, are the inscriptions of the ten commandments, being carved in eight different languages. These guides for living are inscribed in the eight languages of English, Arabic, Chinese, Hebrew, Hindi, Russian, Spanish, and Swahili. The four script texts are Babylonian, Classical Greek, Egyptian Hieroglyphs, and Sanskrit. These were significant in the teachings of occult mystery schools such as Freemasonry and the Rosicrucians.

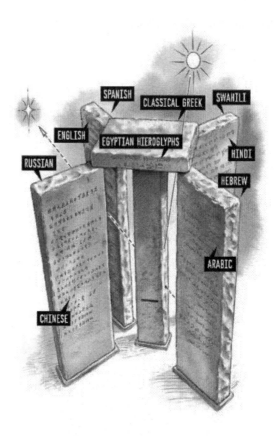

Languages/Texts Of The Georgia Guidestones

It was erected in a configuration pertaining to the migration of the sun's course throughout the year, and its rising and setting. The center column portrays two distinct features, a hole drilled into the center stone so that the North Star could always be visualized at any given time, and the slot was positioned with the rising sun at the time of the solstices and the equinoxes. At the base of the Guidestones, is a tablet that identifies specifications of the structure, such as physical data, astronomical features, sponsors of the project, structural parts in various languages, and a time capsule supposedly buried underneath it. The contents of this capsule are unknown, and the opening date of the time capsule has been left blank and not determined.

ASTRONOMIC FEATURES
1. CHANNEL THROUGH STONE
   INDICATES CELESTIAL POLE
2. HORIZONTAL SLOT INDICATES
   ANNUAL TRAVEL OF SUN
3. SUNBEAM THROUGH CAPSTONE
   MARKS NOONTIME THROUGHOUT
   THE YEAR

AUTHOR: R.C. CHRISTIAN
        (A PSEUDONYN)

SPONSORS: A SMALL GROUP
OF AMERICANS WHO SEEK
THE AGE OF REASON

TIME CAPSULE:
PLACED SIX FEET BELOW THIS SPOT
ON
TO BE OPENED ON

Time Capsule Tablet

There has been much controversial debate concerning the secret interpretations of these messages displayed on the monument. The message engraved states Ten rules for an "Age of Reason" with the subjects addressed as ten commandments strikingly similar to the New World Order Agenda 21, depopulation, one world government, and one world religion. It promotes there is a theory of a link between the world's elite, secret societies, and the establishment of the NWO(New World Order). After the stones were erected, R.C.Christian wrote a book named "Common Sense Renewed" and sent copies of it to all members of Congress, along with other influential leaders.

"Common Sense Renewed" By Robert Christian

R. C. Christian and his organization identities
continue to remain anonymous, but they left behind a text defining the
reasoning behind the rules or commandments of the Guidestones. It is
named the Georgia Guidestones Guidebook,a pamplet produced by the
Elberton Granite Finishing Company, in 1981, which reveals the
interpreted purpose of the Guidestones is to achieve ideal world
conditions, after a catastrophic event. The booklet mentions the fact that
Fendley was a mason as well as many others that were involved in the
monument's construction. Their intentions for the monument is to
expand communication through astronomical phenomena, political and
philosophical natures.

The Georgia Guidestones

Chapter 3 The Ten Commandments/Eight Languages/Ancient Texts

One of the world's great unsolved mysteries is the understanding behind the symbolic reasoning, of the ten commandments of the Georgia Guidestones, supposedly designed to ensure mankind's survival in a post-apocalyptic event. Many researchers associate these principles with the ideals of the New Age thinking, and occult secret societies, that are implementing a New World order of the world's elite, the Illuminati,who believe that too many humans are depleting their natural resources, that they wish to keep and use for themselves only.

The first commandment states to Maintain humanity under 500,000,000 in perpetual balance with nature. As of 2018, the current world population, stands at 7 billion, so this principle suggests an extermination of 9/10ths of mankind, a massive depopulation agenda. This proposal to cull the human population down to a specific number has shocked and alarmed the monument's critics, demanding that the stones be destroyed. The second commandment says to Guide reproduction wisely-improving fitness and diversity. This statement has been interpreted to refer to the structure the number of children allowed per family through selective breeding, once known as eugenics, associated with the Nazis. It suggests that reproduction must be controlled, but by what means, is it government intervention, war, genocide, abortion, etc?

A third commandment is to Unite humanity with a living new language, thus indicative of the process of a one world government. The fourth commandment reads Rule passion-faith-tradition-and all things with tempered reason. The decrypting of this commandment is that the government should determine judicial control over religion and faith issues. The fifth commandment states to Protect people and nations with fair laws and just courts, and the sixth commandment to Let all nations rule internally resolving external disputes in a world court. These two principles imply that it is the government's responsibility to protect all people through a New World order court , a global government should be the overseers of all matters, and not the individual.

The seventh commandment reads Avoid petty laws and useless officials. The determination of the legal code will be interpreted from the viewpoint of the ruling class with the power. An eighth commandment says to Balance personal rights with social duties. This principle referring to an individual's rights taken away for the benefit of the whole social community. The ninth commandment is to acknowledge the Prize truth-beauty-love-seeking harmony with the infinite. This is the effort or movement to replace Judeo-Christian beliefs with a new one world religion. The last tenth commandment states to Be not a cancer on the earth-Leave room for nature-Leave room for nature. This reveals their mind control thinking, as they can rationalize the extinction of nearly all of mankind of the world's population, comparing a human life to being a cancer upon the earth.

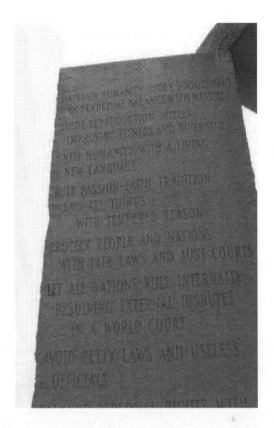

The Ten Commandments Of The Georgia Guidestones

The covert group of R.C. Christian and his organization claim that these ten commandments transcribed on the Guidestones is destined for the remnants of humanity that survives, so that they may use these guides to reestablish a better civilization, and that no nefarious motives or pagan overtones exist behind this monument. If this is true, many people wonder why the need for all the secrecy and anonymity? However, five main categories define the Guidestones's messages according to notable researchers, promoting depopulation and reproduction control, global one world government and court system, one world religion, a new spirituality, and policies of sustainable development or "socialism", and emphasis on man's relationship to nature's resources.

There is a granite tablet placed within a few feet of the Georgia Guidestones which states that "LET THESE BE GUIDESTONES TO AN AGE OF REASON". Many scholars believe that this quote references the classic work attributed to Thomas Paine, an 18th century American Revolutionary. He was a British radical, a deist, that critiqued institutionalized religion, and many felt an attack on orthodox Christianity. Being born in 1737 in England, he immigrated to America in 1774. Paine was a writer and political theorist, and the author of "The Age of Reason", which was a series of pamphlets that were published in three parts, in 1794, 1795, and 1807.

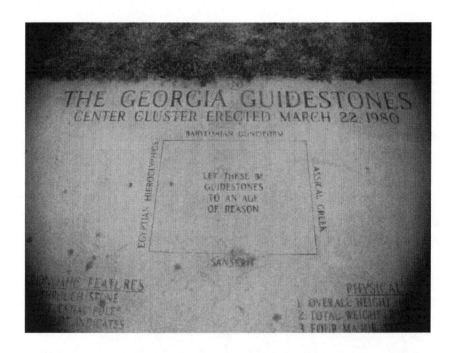

"Age Of Reason" Tablet Marker

As a deist, Paine expressed the theological view that the existence of God is affirmed, but does not believe that he has any supernatural or miraculous interventions with the accordance of the universe. Miracle occurrences were deemed as scientifically impossible. Paine challenged the inspirational teachings of the Bible and opposed all of the world's major religions. His viewpoints did not represent the ideals of the majority of his contemporaries, but resonated with the critics of organized religion, and the atheists.

Paine stated that he believed in God and an afterlife, "I believe in one God, and no more and I hope for happiness beyond this life" in 1794. The primary concepts promoted in "The Age of Reason" were the association of Christianity with mythology, and hearsay evidence, institutionalized church corruption, and the bible being viewed as not the word of God. Paine doubted the legends of Jesus including the Virgin Birth and the Resurrection. He felt they were impossible to prove or disprove based on hearsay evidence, and expecting that the world would believe them based on their claims as in the witnesses to the Resurrection. He promoted deism instead of traditional Christianity, as he believed world religions were corrupt institutions.

According to Paine, he finds the Bible contains internal problems of correlation of events as it is written by human composition, and not the divine word of God. Christians view the Bible as divine revelation from God as transcribed through the written records of the prophets, apostles and Jesus himself. Thus, Paine attacks the fundamental premises of the Christian Churches. Paine enjoyed popularity in Europe and the United States, peaking in America in the mid 1700s. One of his most famous works was "Common Sense" written in 1775-1776, and it promoted his belief that America should be independent of British rule.

Thomas Paine

After Paine's arrival to America, he achieved literary and political prominence, and many associate his success with his close associations to many famous Freemasons, in America, France and England, contending that his philosophy and actions were in conjunction with Masonic ideals and their practices. Some claim he was a leading member of the Rosicrucian fraternity in America, who were recognized as publishing manifestos promoting the importance of world transformations. Paine's essay "On the Origins of Freemasonry" in 1810 was written preceding his death, and many people interpret this as evidence he was a masonic member. It contains the principles and beliefs involved in freemasonry. Others feel that it is inconclusive proof for one way or another.

Numerous conspiracy theories exist concerning the purpose of The Georgia Guidestones in association with the New Age movement. Their ideal world vision is to link the secret occult societies, the elite and the Illuminati, to usher in a New World global order. The ten commandments inscribed on these stones are similar in significance to Agenda 21 for the 21st century. Agenda 21 is a plan for world domination, a one world government, one world religion, depopulation, and the creation of sustainable society development. The plan incorporates all areas of the impact of human life on the environment.

The United Nations System, and large organizations such as The League of Nations, The Bilderbergs, Council of Foreign Relations, and the Trilateral Commission are all pursuing the same goal, to control world governments, and all human life upon the planet. Every aspect of life will be regulated such as resources of food, water, electricity, and transportation. They will be an all seeing eye on individual liberties and there will be no more national sovereignty, everything and person will be regulated and controlled.

Some of the proposed theories regarding the importance of the monument are it portrays a global one world government with a world court that will rule the world. The monument may be built on a power nexus with its core power to be released at an unknown time. The stones convey psychic messages being built on a sacred place next to Native Americans. The site is within ten miles from Ah-Yeh-Lia-Lo-Hee, known as the Cherokee "Center of the World." In ancient prophecy, when the stones are returned to the center of the world, the signs will foretell of the time of the fifth world, a new age according to the Hopi Indians. It is designed by its astronomical features to position celestial bodies , as a gathering place for the worship of dark forces.

Cherokee Center Of The World

The stones are constructed to survive a global apocalypse, with an apocalyptic date surmised a few years back as October 3, 2014, the date has come and passed. The commandments on the stones aid the survivors in the laws that should govern the new world. The more enlightened society will create this New World Order, and avoid overpopulation. Christians view this objective as a call to genocide or a culling of the population, with an intention to create anti-christian sentiment, and the ten commandments of the Antichrist. It is believed that the unknown identity of R.C. Christian, he was a man under the influence of occultism, of Rosicrucians, Freemasons or other secret societies. Speculation has been rampant due to freemasonry symbolism and hidden meanings, and numerical analysis of the carvings on the monument.

Vandalism has occurred with spray painted messages across the inscriptions, and the slabs have been splashed with polyurethane, a more difficult substance to remove than paint. It has been reported that various pagan groups have performed rituals there, with even a cove of witches making pilgrimages there to initiate their ceremonies. On September 11, 2009, a cube of granite measuring 6 inches was taken from the top of one of the Guidestones. It was recovered four years later, as police arrested alleged suspect William Jeremy Ellis attempting to replace that same cube back in the middle of the night.

His claim to the police was that he took it for "personal esoteric and numerological reasons." This notched hole was empty until 2014, when a new cube that was marked with letters and numbers appeared back in the hole. The letters MM were inscribed on the top, with the word JAM on the bottom. The following numbers were carved on the face sides 8, 16, 20, 14. This mysterious cube was placed in the empty indent between the English and Spanish slab.

Mysterious Cube 2014

This updated message on the cube suggested to many that this was some type of warning to mankind, as the occult use numerology often in their messages. The date of October 3. 2014 was considered a possibility as a doomsday event, and the number totaling 666 was arrived at by numerologists conclusions. The letters MM may have been referring to Mason terminology, or as a manufacturer of granite memorial monuments. JAM was surmised as referring to a joint annual meeting that is used by industries including the granite marble industry.

On September 25, 2014, the supposed official groundskeeper removes the cube and destroys it with a hammer and chisel, handing out pieces to onlookers and bystanders. The city installed camera surveillance, and it is currently monitored and updated. In Elberton, the Elberton Granite Museum displays an impressive model of the Georgia Guidestones, accompanied by a short film on its construction. The Georgia Guidestones pamphlet, published by the Elberton Granite Finishing Company details the facts of the monument's history and construction.

In conclusion, this book has explored the secrets behind the origins of the Guidestones, its construction, the ten commandments for the New Age, the "age of Reason" concept, conspiracy theories surrounding the monument, and the puzzling cube of 2014. These intriguing stories present a truly inexplicable unsolved mystery as to their intent and purpose for future civilizations. As conspiracy theories are highly speculative, I encourage all my readers to complete their own research on the subject, to attain knowledge to be aware of possible ramifications for future events, so preparations can be made for themselves, families, and friends, after arriving at their own conclusions.

On a final note, I would like to present striking similarities that exists between the conspiracy theories of the Georgia Guidestones, and the Denver International Airport. Theorists believe that they are both coded symbolic freemasonry imagery, hieroglyphs, and artwork revealing a plan to implement the New World Order, shrouded in secrecy, and both employ a time capsule that is supposedly buried and to be opened at an unknown date. If you have enjoyed reading this book, my book on the Denver Airport is titled "Conspiracy Theories Beneath the Radar The Denver International

Airport".

Made in the USA
Las Vegas, NV
31 October 2021